THE POLAR REGIONS

THIS EARTH OF OURS

Mel Higginson

The Rourke Corporation, Inc.
Vero Beach, Florida 32964

Edited by Sandra A. Robinson

PHOTO CREDITS
© Mel Higginson: cover, pages 4, 7, 13, 21;
© Werner Zehnder/Zeagrahm Expeditions: pages 8, 10, 15, 18;
courtesy Alaska Division of Tourism: title page, pages 12, 17

Library of Congress Cataloging-in-Publication Data

Higginson, Mel, 1942-
    The polar regions / by Mel Higginson.
    p. cm. — (This earth of ours)
    Includes index.
    ISBN 0-86593-378-2
1. Polar regions—Juvenile literature. [1. Polar regions.] I. Title.
II. Series: Higginson, Mel, 1942-   This earth of ours.
G590.H54   1994
574.5'2621—dc20   94-9406
                                                            CIP
Printed in the USA   AC

TABLE OF CONTENTS

THE POLAR REGIONS

The poles are imaginary points at the "ends" of the Earth. The north pole is in the Far North, in a region known as the Arctic. The south pole is in the Far South, at the opposite end of the Earth. The south pole is on the continent of Antarctica.

The polar regions — the areas near the poles — are the Earth's iceboxes. They are extremely cold in winter.

Both polar regions have rugged mountains, lots of ice and amazing numbers of tough animals.

*Packs of sea ice form
on the polar seas*

THE ARCTIC

The Arctic region is not a continent. It is an area that includes the Arctic Ocean and parts of Canada, Alaska, Greenland, Russia and far northern Europe. Arctic land is covered by a "carpet" of low-lying plants called Arctic **tundra.**

Arctic winters are dark and frigid. Spring, however, brings an explosion of plant and animal life. Hundreds of thousands of birds **migrate,** or travel, to the Arctic to nest. Whales migrate to the Arctic seas to feed.

Birds like this golden plover migrate north to nest on Arctic tundra each spring

ANTARCTICA

Antarctica is a continent almost covered by ice and snow. Only a tiny part of Antarctica is fit for living things. Most of those **organisms** are simple plants and tiny animals.

Near Antarctica, though, the islands and seas are rich with life. Thousands of whales and seals live in the Antarctic region. Millions of sea birds, many of them penguins, live there in huge groups called **colonies.**

Visitors to Antarctica find a rugged land of mountains, ice and snow

9

ANIMALS OF THE POLAR REGIONS

Marine, or sea, mammals — whales and seals — live in both polar regions.

No land mammals live in the Antarctic region. However, polar bears, **caribou,** hares, lemmings and musk oxen live in the Arctic.

Both polar regions have huge numbers of birds. Antarctica is famous for penguins, but more than 40 other kinds of birds live in the region, too.

Many kinds of seals
live in the polar regions

An Eskimo in his umiak, *a boat made of animal skin,
looks across the northern polar sea*

A snow goose sits on its nest on the Arctic tundra of northern Canada

HOW ANIMALS LIVE IN POLAR REGIONS

The animals of polar regions have special ways to deal with living in such cold **habitats,** or homes.

Nearly all marine mammals, and some birds, have a layer of fat called **blubber.** Blubber helps animals store energy and stay warm. The blood of some polar animals has a warming chemical in it.

The Arctic fox has short ears and a short nose. That means less of its body is exposed to the cold.

Feathers and a layer of blubber keep Antarctica's penguins warm in the coldest weather

PEOPLE IN THE ARCTIC

Groups of people have lived in the Arctic region for thousands of years. Eskimos are the best-known and most widespread group.

Until recent years, Eskimos lived off the Arctic lands and seas. They had to hunt and fish for most of their food. They made boats of animal skins and weapons from bones.

Today, most Arctic people live with both modern ways and old ways.

Alaskan Eskimos lead a dog team across Arctic ice

PEOPLE IN ANTARCTICA

Until the late 1800s, no one had landed on Antarctica. Whale hunters were the first visitors — but groups of people have never settled in Antarctica. The continent is too windy, cold and **barren.**

The only people who live in Antarctica are the scientists who do research there. Most of the scientists leave this frigid land during the Antarctic winter, each June, July and August.

Visitors tour the great penguin colonies of Antarctic islands

THE ARCTIC COMMUNITY

Think of the Arctic as a neighborhood, or community, of plants and animals.

Arctic plants grow by taking food from soil and sunshine. Some of the Arctic animals, such as hares, lemmings and caribou, eat the plants.

Other animals, with claws and sharp teeth, eat the plant-eaters. A hare that munches greens, for example, may wind up in a wolf's stomach.

Caribou live on Arctic plants of the tundra

THE ANTARCTIC COMMUNITY

The Antarctic is largely an ocean community. Even the animals that spend part of their lives on ice and island shores depend upon the ocean.

In the Antarctic seas, as in all oceans, tiny plants and animals called **plankton** are the basic food. Billions of shrimplike **krill** feed on Antarctic plankton. Many animals, including some fish and whales, grow up eating krill.

The fish become food for Antarctic birds and seals. Some of the birds and seals become **prey** for killer whales and leopard seals.

Glossary

barren (BARE ren) — without much plant or animal life

blubber (BLUH ber) — a thick layer of fat in certain animals living in cold climates

caribou (KARE uh boo) — large, northern relatives of deer; wild reindeer

colonies (KAH luh neez) — groups of animals that live together

habitat (HAB uh tat) — the special kind of area where an animal lives, such as the *tundra*

krill (KRILL) — a shrimplike animal of the Antarctic seas

marine (muh REEN) — of or relating to the sea

migrate (MY grate) — to make a seasonal journey from one place to another

organism (OR gan izm) — any living thing

plankton (PLANK ton) — tiny, floating plants and animals of the seas and other bodies of water

prey (PRAY) — an animal killed by another animal for food

tundra (TUN druh) — the "carpet" of low-lying plants that covers much of the ground in the Far North, or Arctic region

INDEX